random
reflections

JUWON ODUTAYO

ISBN: 978-978-996-642-4

RANDOM REFLECTIONS

DEDICATION

For Ayanfe and Afooreofe

We sat in the living room and watched the highlight of Crystal
Palace match against Tottenham. I remember how animated I was
trying to describe how the striker was waiting for the pass
before he scored the goal.
Immediately, you corrected me and said, "Daddy, he was not waiting!
He was patiently waiting."

Those are moments I live for.
Those are times I don't want to miss with you two. Thank
you for making our conversations reflective.

CONTENTS

INTRODUCTION

When a soccer player scores a goal in the first five minutes of play, the stadium erupts in celebration, the player is ecstatic as he breaks into a frenzied run while his teammates chase after him, jump on him, grab him, and celebrate with him. For a few seconds, they are not encumbered with the thought of the remaining eighty-five minutes left to play in the match. They are not nursing any negative feelings that the tables could turn, and they could lose the match. They are not worried about anything else. Their joy at that moment is the fact that their team just scored a goal. They are so positive that their ability to put in a goal is assurance that victory is certain. They are simply present in that moment and are squeezing out all the pleasure and excitement it brings.

Such are the moments we live for. Those pockets of triumph and celebration at the various stops in the ninety minutes of play that we call life. When they come, we celebrate and savor the joy they bring.

So, celebrate each day's victory without belaboring yourself with when the next win will come or if there is defeat in the future. Stay in your moments, squeeze the joy out of it, reflect on the positives and embrace the lessons.

1

I PROSTRATE BY DEFAULT

When I greet my parents, or any elder, my two hands go down the floor in prostration as a mark of respect. It was how my parents trained me to greet elders from the time I could comfortably walk on my two legs. Also growing up in a culture where that was the norm further cemented it. My long stay in that environment and culture was like an adhesive that glued that mode of greeting. So, my parents started it, the community firmed it up and endorsed it.

My First Lady does the same. She's on her knees before she finishes saying Good Evening, and it's not because her knees are closer to the floor. Before the elder could grab her to restrain her she's gone and, on her way, back. She would not be prevailed upon to do contrary. Her body system is wired so. For the number of years that I have known and known her, she hasn't reviewed it or gotten tired of it. You would think learning and exposure would affect it or modify her, but it hasn't. Her number of degrees, honorary or scholastic, has not affected It. Her travels both locally and internationally has not affected it. They haven't and they wouldn't.

I am an adult now, I have left home, left the village, and traveled a bit. I have met other cultures; I have seen other traditions. But no amount of time spent in these cultures and no excessive introductions made on their customs or practices has been strong enough to undo the settings of how you pay homage to elders and those in authority as ingrained in me from childhood. I admired the other cultures, I acknowledged the diversities, but they only further stirred me to appreciating mine and the trainings I got. The joy that I also have one to share while others eulogize theirs is an added pride.

My pastor is not Yoruba and where she comes from you don't have to go on all fours to greet an elder or show respect. But that has never held me back from expressing obeyance in the posture I know best. Am I aware she is not

Yoruba? Of course! Am I aware she wouldn't mind if I excuse her my 'outlandish' cultural display? I am. So why do I do it? Because something in me makes me feel I will be disrespectful if I don't. And by default, I am prone to satisfy this inner moral compass of mine more than her inclinations for politeness.

Is First Lady aware that her peculiar greeting usually catches her subjects unawares? Maybe. Is she making plans to review it sometime in the future? I doubt. Why? Because somehow it has been locked in her system to pay homage in that manner. She does not know different; she has no first, second or third way, that is the only way she knows. And overtime, she has come to love this way, enjoy this way, and find satisfaction in expressing herself this way.

When we show love or affection, we inherently do so through our default settings. We love in the way we have been culturally programmed and impressionably wired to love. Culturally because that is what we've seen modeled in our culture, society, tradition, or the homes we grew up in. Impressionably because that is what we've heard, read about, or experienced that made strong imprints on us.

And we love in this manner not because we do not

know any other way but because we have somewhat resolved that our way is the best. However, if we found what we have seen modeled repulsive and what we have experienced abusive we grow up trying to run away or avoid anything or anyone that has a semblance of it. Contrarily, if it was pleasant and admirable, we unconsciously begin to look out for it in anyone we consider a love interest.

The same way we consider our cultured show of love and affection ideal is the same way others from another cultural setting have firm beliefs in theirs too. O yes! The same way we feel strongly about our methods is the same way others feel strong about theirs. We all are from one culture or another. We are. All of us. If you didn't drop from heaven with no parentage, you are born into a culture. There was an ongoing preset that you were born into that shaped you. Jesus was born into one too and at a time the customs of His time required Him to pay tax. He simply looked for money and paid. He didn't condemn the practice. He didn't sermonize their request by announcing to them He was God. He simply paid. Either by birth or by community or environment certain idiosyncrasies are associated with your origin that rubbed off on you.

Education, exposure, and conversion may open your mind to growth, adjustments, and upgrade but there's a default setting or cultural heritage that you belong to. It predetermines your attitude, your beliefs, your values and your show of love or affection.

When two persons are therefore in a love relationship, it is normal for them to give and respond to love differently. Their different backgrounds, different trainings, different orientations continue to speak in their attitudes, expectations, and desires. At the beginning of their relationship those differing attitudes form a major part of the attraction and the pull they feel towards each other. The different idiosyncrasies, and the shades of their zest to life create a desire for them to be together. If he grew up where he has been cultivated to be expressive, he is thrilled when he finds one who simply drinks in all drama and vivid showing. He is pulled towards one not only soaks it all in but feel he is one in a billion for the kind of energy he brings. If she had been trained to serve sacrificially, she is overjoyed when she finds one who is needy and disadvantaged. What use is your act of service if there is not avenue to express or display it? And where else can it be loudly displayed if not in a disadvantaged soul? We blossom only in places where we are appreciated and loved. These background formations extend further into their personalities and characters. They become their natural dispositions and are expressed in diverse ways.

Many times, what attracts us in another is the uniqueness they have that we don't. What we admire in another most of the time is the ease with which they are able to do the things we aren't able or wired to do. The things we admire, many times, are the things we are lacking in. What significantly pulls you to another is their uniqueness because that's the area they eventually will add value to the relationship. But overtime, as they grow together and spend more time together, these same sources of attraction become sources of intense irritation. These same differences, after a while, become the very things that tends to pull them apart. It's almost unbelievable!

She is not the outgoing type, and he is outgoing, and she liked him for that. They become a pair and she starts complaining he goes out too much and keeps too many friends.

He likes the fact that she is generous and sacrificial. They become a pair, and he hounds her for giving too much and not working with a budget.

He was captivated by her free-spiritedness and playful disposition, they become a pair and he complains she plays too much and doesn't take anything seriously.

She was all over town about how he is so gentle, so easygoing, ad does not talk much. They become a pair and she is complaining that he is too quiet, and he is slow in making decisions.

Those things you saw at first that drew you in, those things that sparked your connection, after a while, become the sources of your many conflicts. Emphasis on 'after a while.' When this happens, you then begin to work tirelessly to make the other become like you. It becomes your preoccupation to change the person and make them like you. And that only makes the situation worse because if your fixation is making the other person become like you, you will be frustrated. I mean, do you want to go back to their parents, their community, their culture, and undo the settings? When frustration sets in, joy is lost. When joy is lost, you want to quit. Quitting would mean you will start the process with another person again. The 'after a while' will happen again and frustration will set in when you are unable to change them to become like you.

So, what will work?

You get a new job through sheer means of your good grades and very impressive qualifications and all the degrees you have gathered over the years. When you sit at your desk in that new job, do you paste your brilliant results all-around your desk area and flaunt it in everyone's faces showcasing the various institutions you've been to? Do you? When your colleagues disagree with you on a work-related matter, do you snap at them and announce you graduated with a first-class? Do you? When your boss summons you to his office to complain about a transaction you didn't handle well, do you remind him of the various certifications you have and the awards you have received over the years? Do you? I didn't think so. Are your qualifications bad? No! Are your many certifications fake? No. Your credentials got you the job, but they are not sufficient to keep you in. Your qualifications opened the door for you but aren't adequate enough to secure your stay. What keeps you in? A deliberate personal growth and development both in character and attitude. You needed your former to get in, you would need the latter to stay.

How do you manage your uniqueness and differences? A deliberate personal growth and development both in character and attitude. A growth in character calls for balance and understanding of your new status. That you respect it, so you don't lose whatever it is you have. Overdo won't work. Overdo of all the things they admire in you will wear them out after a while. But a healthy balance between your natural settings and acquired traits, a wholesome evenness between background formations and learned behaviors would inject spice and newness to the relationship. Because if you misbehave and continue to flaunt your many degrees and certifications at that new job, they will throw you out in a jiffy and forget how fantastic your CV was. Credentials get you in, growth and personal development keeps you in. Balance is knowing where and when to harness the different energies. Salt is a good seasoning, but you know it is a measured amount of salt and other right seasonings that make the soup tasty and delicious because too much salt will damage the soup.

When you are unwilling to grow and embrace new insights, when you are unyielding and remain set in your 'cultured' ways, you destroy what has great potentials for a beautiful life. The statement, 'this is how I am' has caused many untold losses and threw them in a sea of deep regrets. Some will push their growth and personal development on their partner. They assume it is one of the fringe benefits of being in a relationship. Again, such a behavior could be traced to childhood where the parents or siblings practically does everything for them as a child. They could be last born with several older siblings or an only child that the parents dotted on. They grow up feeling entitled, and it is not surprising for them to harbor such huge expectation of their partner. The sad thing is that though they were raised like that, life would be waiting to throw them some curve balls.

Your personal growth and development is personal. If you do not own it, you are not ready to grow. Find a balance.

Find a healthy balance.

2

I'M LOOKING AT YOUR CREDIT HISTORY

You have come to borrow some money from your bank.

Maybe you are trying to build or buy a house, start your own company, take advantage of an opportunity to expand your business, whatever the goal. When you meet with the bank loan officer, having filled all necessary forms, after all the pleasantries, she drops her head on the papers before her and what is she checking? Your credit. She checks your credit to know if they can trust or believe you when you say you will pay back.

At this point, your words don't count, your fine face don't matter, your sugarcoated-smooth-talker personae won't wash. it's your credit she's staring at, its your credit that's speaking to her. And guess what, she's not looking at the credit of the past seven days or one month, she's checking your history, your records, your pattern through the years. She is going through your files and assessing your credit journey with their institution. All the information she needs are in all the papers and documents before her. If your credit is not convincing, she looks up at you, poker-faced, her voice void of any emotion and she delivers the heart-breaking news - 'Sir, we are sorry, we would not be able to grant you the loan you're applying for.' And that is the verdict. Nothing you say would be strong enough to change their position. You may plead and make promises but your records have informed their decision and that is it.

Why are you upset when I ask for time to go through 'the records' to see your patterns?

Why are you angry because I check your 'credit history' before deciding to commit to you?

Why tag me unspiritual if I choose to trust your patterns more than your sweet promissory notes?

Why look at me like that because I say I am not able to 'loan' you my life?

It's God Who won't consult your past before blessing you. I am still on the journey of becoming like Him. For now, all I see is your 'credit history', and I am sorry 'we can't grant you this loan.' I can't sign these papers. I'm sorry.

You are unaware of the future implications of your patterns. If you had known they would be speaking some day, you probably would have done better. So, can we fix this pattern first? Can we chill and make some cool 'credit' moves? Don't get me wrong, I'm not asking for the type of credit moves Nigerians make when they transfer some huge amount of money into their account just so they are granted a visa. That is a one-off and it is somewhat deceptive, if not fraudulent. Such cannot be trusted; a major decision cannot be made based on it.

I speak of patterns, a repeated practice or habit.

I'm asking for consistent deposits, credible transactions, sustainable business deals that would pan over a period of time - A credible Pattern. I mean, can you make effort and create some new credit history?

You know, that the loan bank officer said No the first time doesn't mean it's forever. When you probably come again, and they see different, it's not impossible they might smile an easy Yes. But in the meantime, please do something about this credit history.

3

I'M NOT RUSHING DOWN THE AISLE WITH YOU

I'm not rushing down the aisle with you

I've seen you happy, I also want to see you sad.

I've seen you jolly, I also want to see you upset.

I've enjoyed your largesse; I'll like to see you broke.

Your achievements are laudable, I want to see you disappointed.

I want to see you when you are stressed out. I want to see you when your meal is delayed.

I want to see you when you are frustrated, I want to see you when you're irritated.

I want to see you when your team loses. I want to see when you are under immense pressure.

I want to see you disagree with your mum; I want to see you say No to your dad.

I would like to see you without.

I would like to see you unguarded.

I would like to see you wait.

I would like to see when things don't go your way.

I would like to see your consistency in devotion to Him.

I will love to see your enthusiasm in serving Him.

It won't hurt to see how you submit to leadership.

It is even more delightful when I know the leader is way younger than you.

No, I'm not negative.

I just want to see you in life's different seasons, I just want to know you in life's many phases.

I just want to enjoy the many flavors with you

I just want to see you in all the moments it brings.

Even if seeing you in all of these isn't sufficient, I would still like to see, regardless. I'm not in a hurry to walk down the aisle with you. Let me see how you even handle that.

4

I KNOW WHY YOU SAID YES

You look at the ring. You look at your mama's face. You look at your friends and buddies. You look at your family. How was he able to make everyone turn up? You look at Tayo and you desire to know how he flew in from Nigeria. You look at Osas and Kelechi, you imagine the work they put in to pull this all up together. You look at your baby sister as she perches in one corner grinning from here to here. You look at the beautiful setting chosen as venue. You look at the breath-taking scenery. You look at how much this would have cost. You look at the smiles on everyone's faces. You look at how anxious they are, waiting with bated breath, just waiting for you to scream Yes!

You look at all these...your eyes return, and you see him. In that micro-mini second, you SEE him. Like a blaze, the entirety of your relationship flashes before you.

You see him. You see what others are not seeing. You see your fights; you see the many flights. You see several unhappy days you share. You see the numerous sleepless nights; you see many wet pillows. You see the off and on threats and abuse. You see the discordancy. You see it all glaring at you. In that micro-mini second you shred off the designer jacket he has on, unbuckle his Gucci belt and wristwatch, pull off his clothes, remove his shoes and you see him for who he really is. And because you see, you know and because you know, you know you want better.

But everyone is waiting. The cameras are well positioned, paparazzi is waiting. They have encircled you now and they are waiting.

You look again.

The ring is beautiful, the atmosphere is redolent. The ambience is exotic. He is still on one knee. Everyone is whispering, Say Yes! Even the guests in the room have joined the party now all looking expectant. The pressure!

Fear grips your heart tight and your feet wobbles. Tears drop and your lips quaver. they think you are overwhelmed with enviable love feelings; they think you are swooned by the public show of affection. But your tears have deeper roots they are oblivious of, your sobbing knows yawning sorrows they would never imagine. And with conflicting emotions you open your cakehole and mumble a gloom- laden Yes. The room lights up. Fireworks! Applause! Celebrations! Everyone rejoices. The video man keeps saving the moment for posterity, the photographer keeps taking his shots for memories, and friends continue to cheer. Many hugs and kisses, several congratulatory messages, plenty to eat and drink, social media will be agog with the news. The posts will gather hundreds of thousands of likes and views. This is what fairy tales are made of.

And everyone is happy, everyone except you.

And no one notices, no one except you.

You manage a smile and chide yourself. Come on, if you weren't that happy with him, you could have said so long time ago and go your separate ways. Why would you wait till now and be a party pooper? So much going through your head as you caress the ring. We will work it out. I will cope and bear. We will seek counselling. It can't be all that bad. I mean, everyone likes him, maybe I'm just being paranoid. It's not that serious. We will be fine. He's a good guy. He has his weaknesses, no doubt, but really, who doesn't? I mean, there are no perfect men out there. So, it's okay. And with all that self-talk, you lighten up and cheer up. You join in the party and laugh with your friends and family as they take turns admiring your rock finger.

****

The party is over now. Everyone leaves now. And it's the two of you now. No cameras. No paparazzi. No lights. No exotic ambience. And as reality settles in on you, so you settle. And you struggle. Days turn into weeks. Weeks crawl into months. And you struggle. At each bus stop for a critical decision, you remember the proposal, you think 'what will people say' and so you reconsider. All the signs scream at you, but you silence them and trod on. You hang in there. You give it another shot. And another shot. And another shot. Till you have no more shots give.

Push comes to shove, and it dawns on you that your once dashing smile has disappeared. You realize your radiance is waning and you desperately want your peace of mind back. You realize you are unwilling to jeopardize your happiness on this altar. So, you ask yourself, 'what do I stand to lose?' You weigh your options. And you discover, nothing, absolutely none of the material comforts and pleasures measure up to peace, joy and self-worth. None of the sporadic make-up dinners is worth an ounce of your dignity and respect. You see the light, finally. So, you gather your courage from all the places they'd been scattered. You turn in the ring with all other fringe benefits and luxuries the relationship provided. And very unlike the proposal, this is solemn, and this needs no shutterbug.

You walk out of the door, lift your head high, take a deep breath in, wait a few seconds, and then let it out. In that one long breath, you know what you gained is incomparable to what you lost. And regardless of 'what will people say?' you know if his presence doesn't make any positive impact, his absence pretty much won't make a difference.

5

HOW SHALL i START AGAIN?

You came when my heart had grown cold. I knew I hadn't always been this way.

But every single time it was crushed to pieces. You came when trust was shattered.

I'd spent all energy in me to keep hope alive. But each time I tried it ended a disaster.

Tade came and chiseled a part. I picked myself up and tried again. Greg came and chiseled a part. I picked myself up and tried again. Ahmad came and chiseled a part. I picked myself up and tried again. Okoye came and chiseled more than enough portion for one person. He was the last straw. I stopped trying.

Then you came.

You came when there was nothing left to love. You came when I had nothing left to give.

You came when my sweetness read negative. You came when all I had was chaff and debris. Great guy, bad timing. I said to myself.

I was cold and distant. I was rusty and irritable. I attacked and hurtled you on many fronts.

I wanted you to leave so badly.

I was eager to add you to the statistics. But you came and you stayed.

You worked me through countless ill-wirings. You stayed despite the cruel stones I flung at you.

Patience was your other name. Stamina was your strong suit. You could have left. But you stayed.

You could have given up. But you didn't.

I'm whole now. I'm healed now. I'm better now. I'm

finer now. I'm nicer now. I'm pleasant now.

No longer lacking. No longer needy. No longer crying. No longer lousy.

But...

Just when I thought our bond would become stronger, I realized you only knew to love a broken me

Just when I thought I was going to fully embrace all of you I realized you were ill-equipped to accept a whole me.

My need was your attraction. My brokenness was your pull.

A damaged me you held dear. A recovered me you couldn't receive. Just when I thought we would be smooth sailing

I realized I was completely losing you.

I'm heart-broken again.

How shall I start again?

6

DO YOU KNOW THEM?

They stare from the audience expecting a blunder. They lurk in the corner waiting for your slip-up.

They patiently wait for a mistake so they can scream 'I told you so.' They jeer at your good times so resolved it wouldn't last for long.

Do you know them?

When they hear your love song, all they see is how they aren't real.

When they listen to your vows, all they think of is how you wouldn't be able to keep them

When they read your epistles, all they conclude is how

you live in a bubble and not the real world.

When they see you two, all they watch for are signs of a crack or a break-up. Do you know them?

You stand to testify; they simulate a smile and judge.

You eulogize about your love; they raspberry at your outpouring.

You dance and celebrate; they shush you and ask you take it easy.

Do you know them?

Everything is run through their gutter-tinted spectacles.

Everything is screened through their sorry and shoddy past.

To them, life has dealt them a great blow

For them, payback means taking you prisoner

They are unable to be in the moment

They do not have the capacity to be present

For their preoccupation is majorly negative.

Their experiences achingly unfavorable

So, they carry their toxicity like a badge wherever they go.

Do you know them?

They would want to muffle your joy with the narrative that tragedy lies ahead They would want to soil your victories just to sell their pessimism.

They would want to recruit you, and have you converted They want you like them. Sour. Bitter. Frustrated. Angry.

They are a sick bunch. They want your bed beside theirs in the sickbay.

Rather than entertain them, comfort and pity them. Rather than regard them, help and pray for them.

They deserve assistance, not engagement. They need amnesty, not appointment.

When you find them, be kind to them.

But never let your kindness be mistaken for approval. For He prepares a table before you...

Live in your moments. Make today count

7

EVER FELT THE PAIN OF A NO CALL?

Have you ever felf the pain of a no call?

When you tried to make the team

When you submitted the proposal

When you auditioned for the role

When you popped the question

When you applied for the job

"We will call you." That's what you were told.

You waited with bated breath.

You waited in pulsating silence.

You waited. You checked your phone.

You waited. You checked the network service.

Your thoughts raced.

Your lungs burned.

Your stomach churned.

But no call.

Ever felt the pain?

But I had long nights of intense practice.

But I made my quotations competitive enough.

But I answered the questions correctly.

But my dictions were on point.

But no call.

Ever felt the pain?

Fear and hope at war within you.

Fear gripping. Hope burdened.

Despair a suffocating blanket.

Sleep a distant friend.

And no call. Ever felt the pain?

And *grrrrrrrrrrrrh,* your phone rings.

You fell over as you made a dash for it.

Toe-bleeding, head-aching, leg swollen,

You pressed the answer button

"Hello." Trying so hard to maintain a calm demeanor.

As you arranged yourself on the seat.

And cleared your throat to sound calm

Alas, it was your buddy at the other end.

Ever felt the pain?

You forced a dry smile with teeth in it.

You suppressed the anger brewing and contained your disdain.

You feigned indifference and endured the mundane gist.

You massaged your throbbing head and cut the line.

Ever. Felt. The. Pain?

No call. No text. No mail. No post.

And your friends asked incessantly,

"Have they called you?"

If only they knew what major turn around this call would make.

If only they knew how much you have waited for this

pie in the sky.

If only they knew how many times you had to answer the same question.

If only they knew how many times you had to give the same answer.

If only they knew.

Silent phones. Empty inbox.

Zilch. Nothing. Absolutely nothing.

And the question remains "Have they called you?"

You would not have to wait too long anymore. The delay is definitely no denial.

Get ready, you are about to be summoned.

And it will be a good one.

Trust does not break itself. Expectations are not met without the intentionality of individuals. If human relations are integral to living, then we must carefully choose those whom we fraternize with and be deliberate about our commitments to them. We cannot keep hopping from one group to another, we cannot keep replacing love interests. Our actions have direct, inevitable consequences, and so does our inactions.

8

PASS YOUR TEST

Have you ever been in a group where you started to feel out of place? This was a group you used to love, you enjoyed your hangouts, you looked forward to your meetings. But things began to degenerate, and it seemed the group could no longer hold. Have you ever been in such a situation? Have you ever been in a relationship where you became so tired? This was someone you used to adore and cherish but as you got closer their flaws became more and more evident and you no longer could deal.

It was a group you'd been for the most part of your life. You used to give one another that energy to dream, that belief that made you get out of bed in the morning and be willing to make the day count. This group had that essence that fired some passion in you.

You two started out as buddies and gradually the connection became deeper and intimate. You both nursed so much hope for future growth and personal development. You shared same beliefs, same values, same purpose, same everything. Iron sharpening iron, prodding one another up towards greatness and wholeness. But then things began to happen, and trust began to wane. You began to watch how lethargy had set in and monotony became the order of the day. You thought it was a phase and it would pass. But it didn't. And when you tried to calibrate the settings, it came back to bite you.

The group began to diss one another and tear each other apart. This wasn't what you bargained for, you thought. You didn't envisage you were going to arrive here. Backbiting. Bitterness. Bad blood. The same values you once held high they began to denigrate. The same messages they preached, push came to shove, and they rubbished it. And the annoying part was they became defensive, they became militant. They began to trade years of building trust and friendship for crazy moments of unbridled madness. And the walls came crashing down. The group no longer could hold, the friendship lost its footing. And for a minute, you were stunned, you looked at yourself, and wondered if you were putrid or if you did something wrong because you desperately wanted explanation on how things could flip so quickly. The meetings became bland and tasteless. The hangouts lost its soul. And now everyone sat in silence, but they were screaming obscenities at each other without saying a word. It was time to leave.

The pattern is the same whether in a group of ten or twenty friends as it is in a love relationship between a man and a woman. The closer you get to people, the clearer you see their inadequacies. The more time you spend with friends, the more you know them and the more obvious their flaws and shortcomings. And the more they see yours too because all men are fallible. Disappointments come from unmet expectations. And distrust is the product of botched promises. Teaching is easier than practice. Every time you open your mouth to share your opinion on issues or declare your stand on certain delicate subjects, and you wax lyrical about it, occasion would soon demand you to walk the talk.

All friendships and relationships go through test. As two people continue to interact, opinions will clash, claims and assertions will be tested. The day you teach about Forgiveness, that same day, your test is prepared. The day you stand up to speak about Sacrifice, that same day, the stage is set, the characters are developed, and the settings arranged for your test. The day you condemn Cheating, that same day the lady or man with your specifications gets on stage. The test may not be conducted in a month or two, it may not be conducted in four or five years, but it will definitely hold. You should not be ignorant; it should make you tread cautiously. Because every day, each scene is developed, each act leads to the other and everything leads to that final day. When that test finally shows up, it's with a bang, it will shake the very foundations of your value systems. It will rock the faculty of your being. You would feel like you are walking through the valley of shadow of death. You would wish you never made commitments. You would wish you never shared your strong feelings on issues.

If you pass your test, the same power it possesses that makes it sufficient to break you, that same power will revolutionize your world and place you on a pedestal that would be impossible for your adversaries to deny. If you pass, you make little effort, and you get a bumper harvest. You talk little and the resounding effect will deafen someone a thousand kilometers away. Church folks call it anointing. I'll like to call it, Overtop. Your FIFA ratings would be over the top. Your partner would be willing to go to any length for you. When you call one, thousands will answer and run before they even hear what the errand is. It's the reward of passing your test. It's Overtop. (And of course, it automatically raises the expectation bar again.)

But if you fail your test, you dent the fiber of friendship and sear the layers of relationships built overtime. You shatter into tiny, tiny pieces every block of loyalty and integrity you painstakingly built over the years. The more you fail your test the more you destroy the permissible layers of absorbing the morals and teachings. Every failure keeps peeling it away, every gullible break in trust and more layers gets peeled. And a time comes when there's nothing left. When that time comes and you talk again, you discover your words bounce back at you. And no matter how much energy you expend and no matter how much you sweat in the air-conditioned room, the words still would bounce back at you. And at that moment, it becomes evident, the pillars of friendship can no longer hold.

Every time you talk, make an assertion, declare your opinion on a matter, you raise the bar of expectations. The level of expectation placed on you is determined by your closeness to the person, the frequency at which you talk, and your consistency in disapproving wrong behavior. And the frequency of your contact with someone is directly proportional to the rate at which you talk, share your opinion, and assert yourself. However, the more you assert yourself, the more you are susceptible to error and the more your flaws become visible.

After a while you become weathered by the scorching sun of distrust and botched promises because of your closeness to a person. You become wearied by loads of unmet expectations and acute disappointments. It's reason people who are closer to you hurt you more than acquaintances. It's reason why seemingly insignificant issues become the fibers broken relationships and broken marriages are made of. It's reason people are puzzled when you tell them how it all ended. And they go, 'you mean that was what happened?!'

If you've been friends for four years, if you've been buddy-buddy for six, if you've wined and dined for eight years and you've been in each other's faces for ten, don't pick offence when they expect certain behaviors from you and don't shrink if they anticipate your idiosyncrasies. If you've been dating for two years, if you've been married for ten, don't recoil when they assume you would act in some certain ways and don't feign surprise if they are shocked when you don't. You trained them so, you played them so, unfortunately unconsciously. Time spent with you wired them like that. Years of listening to you, laughing at your not so funny jokes, chitchatting, and playing video games together did that to them.

Therefore, awareness is key. It is important you know that nothing just happens. Trust does not break itself. Expectations are not met without the intentionality of individuals. If human relations are integral to living, then we must carefully choose those whom we fraternize with and be deliberate about our commitments to them. We cannot keep hopping from one group to another, we cannot keep replacing love interests. Our actions have direct, inevitable consequences, and so does our inactions. Some friendships go through the time-test and are broken, some others go through the same time-test and become stronger. Time would test everything. The question is, when the tests come, would you pass?

When the tests come, will the group disintegrate? Will the story be The Agony of what we used to have? When the test come, will your relationship fall apart? Will your story be The Wretchedness of what used to be? He says, "I will never, never ever, put on you more than you can bear." I Corinthians 10:13. That only means you can pass your test. You have the capacity to pass your test.

HOW MANY DATES DO YOU NEED?

How many dates do you need before knowing this is it?

How many dates should a guy and girl have before declaring exclusivity? One date? Two dates? Three? Five?

I mean, some guys take a girl out on a date, and they believe that since she chose to come out for the date, it is a done deal that they both are a pair. As in, since she came out for the date, she has automatically become a girlfriend. And the girl wonders, 'just because I ate a plate of Jollof rice and drank a bottle of Coke that you paid for, am I now your girlfriend?' Does that mean she is a girlfriend to every dude who buys her lunch or dinner?

Oh well, a flip question would be, do you need to eat 4 or 5 plates before he can tag you his? How many plates of Jollof rice do you need to eat and how many bottles of Coke do you need to drink before he can lay claim to you? How many plates? How many dates?

For some, one date is all they need to know that this is not it, that they can't do this, that this is absolutely not for them. One date. Just one date! It will shock you how much you can know and gather in one date. So, for some people, one date is enough. And they will tell themselves, 'Sweetheart, you can't deal. This is not for you.'

It may be from something he said or something she didn't say, it may even be from the way he eats the rice or the way she speaks to the waiter. And so, 30mins into that one date they've heard something, they've seen something, they've noticed something, and they just know like they know their name is John or Sharon, that they wouldn't hang around here. One date.

That's why some people make an effort to put their best foot forward in a first meeting! That's the reason! Because you may never get a second chance to make a first impression.

Come on, think about it, look at the way you suit up and dress correctly for a job interview. You make sure you look sharp and clean just so you could impress your interviewers. For many, a first date isn't different, it is like a job interview. You never can tell what your interviewer is looking for, so you put your best foot forward, so you win the job – the guy or lady. I call this category of people, *One-Shotters*.

One-Shotters - they are men, who start out defining it from the onset. They tell you oh ha from the first date, that they like you and they are interested in you. In fact, they tell you before the meal for the date is served, no dilly-dallying, no jiggery-pokery. They let you know straight off they didn't come out because they were hungry or thirsty, the meal is not the priority, you are and getting to know you is. So, they drop it there at your table, they couldn't be bothered by all the calculations and permutations of 'should I or should I not?' They just say it, drop the mic and let you take your time and make your decision. Not until they pour out their minds would they feel free to look at their meal. There are men like that – *One-Shotters.*

It probably looks sweet to meet such a man who is that straightforward, who knows doesn't just know what he wants but goes right ahead to communicate it. Sweet, right? But, the irony of life is, while some lady would consider such out rightness in a man to mean focus, responsibility, readiness, and decisiveness, while some lady would consider such out rightness a positive sign, while some lady find such sincerity in a man attractive (like, this is what I'm looking for, after these many years with men who just wanted to play around and waste precious time, to see a man who says it straight from the shoulder on the first date is rare, uncommon and heaven-sent) while some lady would thank their God and say their search is over, some other ladies see this out rightness on a first date as pressure. Search me! The irony of life! To some lady that's pressure! Such ladies are, 'hey, slow down, take a chill pill, dude. Can we just enjoy the moment? Can I enjoy this Jollof and drink my juice in peace? Can we just take things easy for now?' Some ladies will see it as pressure. Talk about different strokes for different folks.

To some people, such decisiveness on a first date is too much tension and stress. And I'm thinking, could their response be linked to the fact that they are still young, foot-loose and fancy-free? Could their response be because of the fact that they believe they still have so much time on their hands and would like to just chill and catch some fun? Well, it's not impossible.

Then we have the 2nd category of people.

Additionals - For these ones, one date won't cut it. For them, he still seems fuzzy, she is still mysterious, there's just something about him/her they can't figure, and they know they will need more time, more opportunities, more dates before they can make a decision. There are people like that. There are people who feel all you do on a first date is to impress and make an impression just like a job interview. All the right words you say, the courtesies, the niceties are just a facade, and not the real you. They believe that if they give you more time, more meetings, more dates, your true colors will come out. Such people are *Additionals*. They need additional date, additional hangout, additional movie time, additional phone call, additional time.

They just don't come out feeling it hot and strong from the beginning. And the issue isn't that they are young or footloose and fancy-free, they simply are like the microwave, it takes time for them to warm up and latch onto the vibes you throw at them. They are just wired like that. One or two dates won't do, it's too small to make a major decision like that. They like to wait and see consistency and credible patterns. They want to have a better, sure ground to build trust on. For them, one date does not provide that sure ground or foundation. They want more, they want an addition to the first or second date. They are not slow starters. They are *Additionals*.

Whether one date or ten dates, you want to be sure you know to a certain level what you are signing up for, the key point to note is that you both must take time out to get to know each other. Just the two of you asking questions and answering. You may choose to prioritize quality over quantity but never forget that patterns need room and time to evolve.

10

DISPOSABLES

Disposable cups. Disposable plates. Disposable spoons. Disposable napkins.

Who wants to be bothered with an extra cost of washing hundreds of dishes after the event is over?

Who has time to spend too much time cleaning and packing?

So you have them in various shades and forms (plastic or paper) and for whatever purpose or function you desire them.

Our penchant for not wanting to carry load draw us to them.

Our zero- tolerance for stress makes us choose them.

No weight. Never a burden.

They are designed to be used just once.

They are configured for lone operations.

And when you are done with them, into the trash can they go.

It's how we have made people become.

Disposable friendships. Disposable members.

Easily forgotten. Easily discarded.

Easily replaceable. 'No one is indispensable.'

The speed with which we get rid of them.

The manner with which we throw them away.

We're the 'Moving-On' generation.

We're the 'No-Time' subgroup.

We Mooove!

Once their opinion is different, we withdraw.

Once they're becoming difficult, we dispose them off.

Once their views misalign with ours, we lose their seat at the table.

Once they say No to our demands, we dump them in the bin.

Once they turn down our request, we disenfranchise them.

That's why you can't mention the disposed in their circles again.

You dare not refer to them in their meetings.

Everything they have been, everything they have done is reckoned dead.

Ten years friendship gone. Twenty years relationship perished.

Like even the good times you had with them suddenly become outlawed.

It's how we've made our relationships become.

Disposables!

Plastic relationships. Paper marriages. One quarrel, we threaten to leave.

One disagreement, we ex them.

One altercation, they are in the trash can.

One misunderstanding, we carry our load.

Like it's now a crime to hold a divergent view.

Like it's felony to be an individual.

Disposables.

But You didn't raise us like that.

You're always seeking us out.

You're always pioneering the chat.

'Adam, where are you?'

'Cain, why are you angry?'

'Hagar, where are you going?'

'What are you doing here, Elijah?'

'Moses what's in your hands?'

'Woman, will you give Me water?'

You will call. You will ring.

"Come let's reason together."

Come let's talk it over.

Though our differences be like dividing walls.

We can leverage on each other's uniqueness for strength.

You're never abandoning.

You're always remembering.

Authoring a ceasefire. Initiating engagement.

Ever more bothered we're gone.

Ever so ready for reconciliation.

*

Demola, where are you?

Chidi, why are you angry?

Eseosa, can we talk?

Samuel let's meet for dinner.

Let's have this conversation.

Let's mend the bridges.

11

TO FORGIVE

What do you do when their Sorry does not translate to a change in character? What do you do when their apologies do not yield fruits of repentance?

You give forgiveness to restore the relationship again. It is a poise to want to trust and relate again. You are confident that lessons have been learned and things will be better. Forgiveness means you are willing to let your guards down once more, being confident you will not be shot at again. And that even if you are, at least, it should not be in the same place they have been sorry.

If you have your shield about you, if you fence yourself in, if you circle your space and territory, you may truly not have forgiven. You could successfully fence yourself in if the party is just a friend. You could successfully guard your territory if they are just allies who have no special stake in your life. And they will not even notice your carapace if you do that. You both could carry on like everything is hunky-dory. The fact that they are not in your face 24/7 is an advantage. You have some level of control over how much access you give them. You can preempt your meeting and interactions and as a result prepare ahead of time your reactions, your remarks. You can fake your smiles; you can stage excitement and simulate laughter. Your antennae are all about you and you know your acting would be over in a couple of hours or more and the whole shebang will be all over. You may do that with a random friend.

But how do you successfully do that to your partner, your spouse, when you know they are going to be in your face 24/7? How do you forgive and still fence yourself in? How can you successfully do that? For how long can you put up an act or show? For how long can you be plastic and pretend?

How do you forgive them and not let down your guards again? How do you forgive, and you still are not able to laugh wholeheartedly and smile genuinely? How do you forgive a spouse and still have your shields about you? How do you create space and boundary in the same space you two are housed in and claim you have forgiven? In a marriage?

To forgive is to restore to status quo. It is to laugh hysterically with them like you used to, chat with careless abandon like you used to, play with childlike vigor like you used to.

To forgive is to not be conscious of the hurt again and to not remember the point of pain again.

To forgive is to believe there will be change in behavior.

To forgive is to trust their apologies will yield fruits of repentance.

To forgive is to risk the arrow of hurt will not be shot again.

To forgive is to dare to be

-     vulnerable again

-     exposed again

-     unguarded again

-     unarmed again

-     preyed on again

To forgive is to gift yourself the opportunity to

-     love again

-     laugh again

-     live again

-     joy again

-     be whole again

To forgive is to choose

growth over stagnancy

freedom over subjection

joy over despondency

hope over despair

To forgive is to look beyond the apology and how the Sorry is packaged and choose your peace of mind. It is to refuse to hand over the control of your mental state to the offender and own the conversation.

To forgive is to choose you, and everything that choosing you entails.

12

UNSPOKEN SURENESS

It takes a lot of courage for anyone to be vulnerable when they are starting out with another.

It takes a huge amount of confidence to take the risk and reveal any part of ourselves in what could be a love relationship.

Even when the other makes us comfortable in their presence and our nuances seem to come out naturally, we still seem guarded.

How much should I let go? How much should I reveal?

And every meeting presents us with an opportunity to reveal a little more, open another layer and put ourselves out there.

But when that opportunity comes, we become afraid, and we dillydally. Do we hold back, or do we let go?

We are simply seeking for some unspoken sureness. Our souls yearn for some assurance.

We look for it in their expressions.

We search for it in their passive remarks. We look for it in their casual gestures.

We search for it in their stare, their glance, and their calculated silence.

Love is the sureness that your vulnerability is safe in the hands of another.

The dude buried the one talent because he was afraid. He kept it for fear. Same way many of us keep our feelings for fear. We keep our emotions for fear.

Fear that it would be trampled upon. Fear that it would not be reciprocated.

You don't want to show too much, for fear. You don't want to give too much, for fear. You don't want to laugh so hard, for fear.

You don't want to appear you like them, for fear.

So, you bury your essence, you bury your you, for fear. Until you can find that unspoken sureness, that unquestionable and unerring confidence that you will be safe.

You are not asking them to verbalize it. You are praying you would see it.

You are not demanding they tell you.

You are just wishing they will let it show.

Because to love is not just to risk but to risk it all. For love that is halfhearted and guarded is not love at all.

I pray you find your Unspoken Sureness. Not in the walls of a building, nor in the edifices and structures that are fleeting, but in the deep recesses of your soul, in the certainty He guarantees in all our uncertainties.

13

CHASE

Okay, you like each other, you are fond of each other, so you marry, you go out on dates, you do movie nights, you buy stuff, you make sweet love, you make cute babies, you eat, you go to work, you come back, you make more money, you travel, you buy more stuff, you visit friends, you eat, you make some more love, you sleep, you make more babies, you do more hang outs, you watch more movies, and you eat again, you make more money, you sleep, you wake up....and, and that's all?

As in, that's all?

For the next 40, 50, 60 freaking years that you hopefully will be husband and wife, that's all? You really mean, that's all? Naaaahhhh....God is not that boring! It has got to be more than that. It has got to be for something better and bigger. It must be for something bigger than you. I mean, He is an Intentional God. He can't be so bereft of ideas or creativity as to design this to be a waste. Just to eat and drink? Come on!

For Abraham and Sarah - An epic lesson in sacrifice. He wanted a nation. He needed a people. It was bigger than them.

For Amram and Jochebed, Israel was the goal. Pharaoh would be stubborn. Moses was in the plan. It was bigger than them.

For Jacob and Rachel, Egypt was in the picture, Famine had been predicted. Joseph had to be sent ahead.

For Boaz and Ruth, one of my faves. Naomi had to be pressed to go back home. Then He crafted a beautiful story of unselfish devotion with Ruth, hence redefined love. By that, He created a prototype of the Kinsman Redeemer. It was a bigger plan.

For Aquila and Priscilla, the early church had to be established. Apollos and Paul needed some heavy moral and financial support. Some cool funds would be key essentials to propagate the gospel. They were designed for such purpose.

For Joseph and Mary, there was a script; you and I were in it. Joseph's tantrums wouldn't be strong enough to stop it. Jesus had to be born. Jesus had to go to the Cross.

They all ate and drank. They all slept and woke up. They all hung out and played. They all took a turn among the cabbages. But then they still got up and worked the script.

So, the movie nights, the dinners are only what they are - special Interludes and exciting Commercial Breaks. The vacations and getaways are simply relished moments of comic bathos, luscious cruise for any grand tour. There is a bigger plan. There's an intent. There's a plot to the movie.

And when you find it, you chase it.

Picnics are cool interludes that make you enjoy the ride.

Dinner dates are stylish breaks that make the trip euphoric and blissful. Great businesses make room for legit luxurious living.

And baby-making, oh sweet baby-making, that is always a mysterious layer in the assignment.

Your love story has a script.

The union is for something bigger.

This merger is for a bigger takeover.

For He said "One will chase a thousand, and two, ten thousand.

And I'm so glad He said one will chase a thousand.

So even without a second, there's still a chase.

So, when you are done eating, please dust your bum and chase.

When you are done shaking the sheets without music or responding to the service of Venus, please put on your cloths and chase.

When you are back from touring the world, unpack and get ready to chase some more.

Even if your wallet is like an onion and every time you open it, it makes you cry, beat it and chase.

On days you are full of spirit as a gray squirrel, Chase.

On days despondency clings to you like a wet garment, chase. Be all softness, beautiful and dominant as the sun, chase.

Be all blue and the weight in your walk is seen by all, chase.

Whether the economy changes with the rapidity of a kaleidoscope, chase. Or is it as dynamic as the English and Spanish leagues, chase.

After the commercial breaks, Chase!

14

SOCCER HAS VAR

In soccer, there's a referee and there are assistant referees. But the game was still prone to error, most devastating and heart-breaking errors. Goal-line technology was introduced. It wasn't enough. Then came VAR! GBAM! Nothing a player does on the field of play now that will not be judged or reviewed.

In tennis, there's a referee, a chair umpire and line umpires. But the game was still prone to error, most devastating and heart-breaking errors. Matchdetermining shots were being misjudged. Championship points carelessly misread. Then Hawk-Eye was introduced! GBAM! A line-calling system which traces a ball's trajectory and sends it to a virtual-reality machine.

In Rugby, there's TMO – Television Match Official. In NFL, there's RRS – Replay Review System. In Cricket, the naked eye of the on-field umpire has been replaced with the hawk-eye of ball-tracking software.

The intention is accountability. The awareness that you are answerable to a system whenever you are on the field of play. Knowing that your actions will be judged, on (and off) court.

Your relationship needs VAR!

Who are you accountable to? What system do you have in place to checkmate your excesses and ensure fairness? Does he have an authority over him you can go to if he misbehaves? Does she have a leader over her you can call if push comes to shove? Your relationship needs VAR! Your marriage needs a Hawk- Eye.

Of course, a soccer match can run its course and VAR is not used throughout. A tennis match can be completed without the need for Hawk-Eye but the consciousness that they are there gives you assurance for objectivity and fairness. And that is simply gratifying.

Be wary of that man who has no one in his life whom he respects and who can call him to order. Be very cautious with that woman who listens to nobody and who nobody can talk to. Many do not want a 3rd party and that sounds good and reasonable. But good and reasonable does not equal to mutual respect and fairness. Good and reasonable does not prevent abuse or cure violence.

Your relationship needs VAR!

So, whether it be 22 or 2, fairness has the same language.

Whether it be short-term or long-term, equity knows no gender.

Soccer has VAR.

Tennis has Hawk Eye.

What does your relationship have?

Soccer has VAR.
Tennis has Hawk Eye.
What does your relationship have?

15

FOCUS ON LITTLE DAILY

Vacation in Miami with your significant other or dinner in a 5-star hotel has all shades of awesomeness.

A summer trip to Disney World or a boat cruise in Dubai on your birthday is definitely nourishing for any relationship.

Basking on the white sand beaches at the Maldives in your own private paradise is incredible and memorable.

A hike through the lush mountains in Hawaii with a private dip in the waterfalls is quite unparalleled and sensational.

Exotic beaches, beautiful sunsets, romantic restaurants, luxury resorts. Amazing feeling. Beautiful memories. But as much as these outlandish gestures are cool, they aren't sufficient to sustain a relationship.

Do as many of them as you can but when you return it would matter to be consistent in little things because...

▪ one intensive annual cleaning of your teeth at the dentist is good for your teeth but when you get up from bed the following morning, it's the DAILY brushing of your teeth that keeps your mouth consistently clean.

▪ one yearly long marathon with your community sport group may be rewarding to your body but it's DAILY exercise that would really make you lose weight and stay fit.

▪ one hour prayer monthly is great and remarkable but a 5mins prayer DAILY builds a stronger relationship with God and is more effective.

It's the DAILY consistent small acts of kindness that keep our relationship thriving and healthy, not the huge overblown gestures of romantic love.

You can go on boat cruise, you can party in Dubai but when you return, still be able to take a stroll together in the evening, make meals and wash the dishes together, send a random text message during the day to check how they are, say I love you without being coerced, serve a morning cup of tea, iron a dress, say Thank you for meals given, bills paid and errands run.

Lavish them with love and be effusive in your praise.

Give encouraging words for projects they embark on; ventures they are involved in and causes they are passionate about. These small gestures should be commonplace! These smaller acts of kindness have a cumulative effect and weigh far more than once-in-a-while glamorous gesture of romantic love.

Focus on little daily.

16

CLICK UPDATE

Companies have induction programs for their new employees. Organizations draw out training plans for their staff.

Businesses design standard technical courses for their teams. Corporations go on annual retreat to regroup and strategize.

These institutions do these, even though they know your stay isn't eternal.

Amazing how we treat the marriage institution we consider permanent differently.

We profess it's forever, but we recess at the sight of training.

We admit we are fallible, but we legit make no effort to do better.

We cause one another pain but will not take courses that will abate them.

We legislate against abuse, but we refuse to update our learning on preventive measures.

We continue to use prehistoric methods to address contemporary issues. Resolve a 3-month premarital counseling is okay to carry a 40 or so year marriage journey.

And we marvel when many fall into depression, and several are suicidal. We wonder why separation and divorce rates continue to rise.

We forget that even a phone app crashes when several notification updates are ignored.

It's been 5, 10 years or more on this 'marriage app'

The promptings for update or a roundtable have been unending.

The warning signs to refine the system and review the progress have been clear. Alerting you to upgrade from the inaugural to an enhanced version.

Drawing your attention to your spouse's concerns, complaints, and fears.

But then the notification comes with two options: UPDATE or IGNORE.

What are you going to do?

87

17

LONG DISTANCE RELATIONSHIP IS NOT FOR BABIES

Ever been down and out and you needed to let out to your significant other? You make the phone call, and you couldn't reach him/her. Several things could be responsible:

poor connection,

network problem,

they are busy at work,

they are indisposed, or

they just are unavailable.

It happens in all relationships. It's more frustrating in Long Distance Relationships (LDR)

What makes a relationship romantic? The moments you share together, the smiles, the long stare into each other's eyes, the laughter, the hugs, the date nights, the movie nights, holding hands, taking walks, etc. The list goes on.

LDR robs you of all that. It denies you of the little funny things that tickle you about your partner. It takes the romance out of it and what you have left in your hands could best be described as friendship. When you are miles apart away from the one you love, the relationship is more akin to friendship than a romantic one.

You have to deal with the fact that they will hang out with other friends in your absence. That they are not being in the same time zone with you could also mean your feelings would not be in the same time zone. You must deal with the fact that you can't make a dash to where they are on impulse to sort out issues. You must deal with unfavorable time differences – your bedtime may be when they are gussying up for work.

If any relationship requires work, commitment, and sacrifice, with all the periodic fights, mood swings and comic bathos, LDR requires all that raised to the power of ten, not forgetting to add affection, patience, understanding, care, high-level effort, unequivocal devotion, unwavering trust, and rock-solid maturity. Being several miles apart is emotionally stressful and energy-draining. You need stamina, you need dogged faith. So, I dare say, LDR is not for babies.

Have you placed a phone call to the one you love, and the network service keeps playing games with your heart? He is finding it difficult to hear you. She is having a hard time making a complete sentence without the connection breaking.

Or you call having had one of the most stressful days and all you could hear at the other end is the laughter and merriment in the background. You could tell he is having a swell time, without you. His animated voice immediately irritates you for no just cause. What right does he have to be laughing and playing when you've just had the most demanding day ever?! How dare him make merry without you?! Unpardonable offence!

Or you call needing encouraging words and she sounds so off and passive, probably because she is also needing a shoulder at that moment to lean on. Ever seen two needy people trying to have a normal cordial conversation? It's rusty!

Or you reach out desperately wanting to share a very exciting hot gist and he goes, 'Dear, I'm a bit busy right now, please let me call you back.' And your balloon just fizzes out, all the effervescence disappears. Because you know too well that the call may not be returned. And if eventually it is returned, you may no longer be in that eager phase again.

Or you reach out and she is just drowsy, and you could feel the tiredness in her voice. You really want to talk but she is coming in and out of the convo because she is sleepy. What do you know, perhaps she left home 5am and came back 11pm? She only managed to make herself some tea for dinner. She had just done that and was pulling the covers over her head when your call came in and you were in high spirits.

Or you are in the middle of that all-important phone conversation, and you have gotten to a point that requires a response from the other side after your lengthy brief, and they suddenly go quiet on you. And you are like, 'Hello? Are you there?' 'Why are you quiet?' 'Am I boring you?' 'So, for all I've said so far, you don't have anything to say?' 'Why are you not answering me?' 'Are you listening to me at all, or you're doing something else?' And like that, just like that, a pleasant gist time, a cordial phone conversation, goes south and everything becomes distasteful, and the evening turns sour.

It's the weight of LDR.

It's nerve-racking when the little time you have to communicate is spent fighting or quarrelling. At the same time, if he is your significant other, you feel it's important you let him know if anything is bothering you. And you know if you let it slide it could grow to become a bigger issue. So, you're caught between I don't want to bother him and I don't want it to be a bother later on.

How many times have you ended a phone call on a sad note, and you are wondering, 'What did I do wrong? What did I say?' 'I only asked a question, I just wanted to know' 'But I was listening, it was only a cough.' Because with LDR, a simple cough at a wrong time is potent enough to cause glitches. No matter how much precious minutes you spend trying to defend the innocence of your cough, it does not change the fact that your partner could go to bed investigating the cough. And this investigation could last for days and the two of you will not say Hello to each other for those days while the investigation is ongoing.

Sometimes the fact that you may not always get to see the expressions on their faces as you talk is painful. You are left with your mind or imagination to believe she smiles when the gist requires smiling and he is sad when the conversation demands pity. So sometimes you find yourself accusing them of not responding appropriately because you are 'smart' enough to tell the expression on their faces just by hearing their voices. *Grrrrrrrrrrhhhhh.* It's the burden of LDR.

That explains why you ask immediately they pick the call, 'what are you doing?' 'Where are you?' 'Are you sitting down?' 'Who is there with you?' 'What are you eating?' 'Whose voice did I just hear?'

Because creating the mood and atmosphere they are in, in your imagination, is important to you. It will inform you to decide if the moment is right for any important message or the gist you want to share.

Again, you may ask these questions innocently in a bid to know if they are in a space to talk, and they take it the wrong way and go, 'Why are you asking where I am?' 'Why do you want to know where I am?' 'Are you stalking me?' 'What are you insinuating, that I am not at home when I say I am?' 'Why are you always asking where I am and what I am doing?' And like that, what should have been a good talk time is messed up.

Relationship is work; Long Distance Relationship is more work. Relationships require effort, Long Distance Relationship requires even more effort. And it is so not for babies. It is not! It is for two mature people who have grown well enough to explore the values and gains of having to live miles apart (temporarily). It is important they have taken roots in before any situation demands the inevitable distance created between them. So, it is also not healthy for newly started relationships. If you just started and LDR happens on you, it's risky. Because if your presence hasn't made any real impact, your absence won't make any real difference.

And no, absence doesn't make the heart grow fonder in LDR, it makes the heart tread through the valley of the shadow of death. If you are married, absence means lonely nights and pillow clutching. If you're single, it means you asking yourself time and time again if it's worth it. 'Shouldn't I leave whatever I'm doing here and relocate? Is it worth it? Is it worth all the traveling expenses, late night calls and data usage? Is it worth all the fights and quarrels?' No, absence doesn't make the heart grow fonder in LDR. It makes the heart weigh options and consider alternatives. It makes the heart go through conflicting emotions.

So, does LDR work? Of course, it does! But you must first settle it within yourself, LDR is not for babies. If you've done that, then these tips would help:

1.   You are the one who would make it work. YOU make it work. You make the effort. It must be mutual, though.

2.   Plan regular visits.

3.   Consider it a phase in your relationship that is temporary and not permanent.

4.   Cut down on your expectations. They won't always be there, deal with it and grow up.

5.   Decide how long you would be apart, put a timeline to it and look forward to the date.

6.   Update each other on your schedules. It will prevent disappointments.

7.   Video-call a lot.

8.   Daily communication (not necessarily daily phone calls) should be a priority. Text messages, IMs, emails, telephone calls, or video chatting, etc. Take advantage of the advancement in technology and social media. The platforms are there, Facebook, WhatsApp, Skype, Instagram, Snapchat, etc. Share photos, share videos, send voice messages, do all that you can and communicate.

9.   Routine is cool but spontaneity could be fun. Even if you have your schedules, like you chat or call at a particular time in the evening, make allowances to be spontaneous sometimes. Just make sure your LD partner is on the same page with you.

10.   If you call several times and there is no response, no need to fret, you're not being ignored. They will call back when they are able. Unless of course you have sown a similar seed, you may just be reaping the fruits.

11.   When (not if) you have misunderstanding, it is not the end of the world. When nails grow long, we cut nails, not fingers. Give yourselves benefits of the doubt and let go. Let the long distance make you more forgiving.

12.   LDR calls for trust. If you sign up to do LDR, then be ready to give unreserved trust. Throw your silly insinuations away, bury all the jealousies and believe the best. You signed up for it, remember?

13.   When they come downloading all the details about how their day went, snap out of whatever 'not-this-time-mood' you are in and just listen! Take a deep breath, get in the groove with them and listen. It is your cross, carry it.

I'm sure you don't want another person to carry it for you. Because if you dare allow another soul to carry it consistently, I guarantee you that is your relationship going down the drain. Do a quick self-talk, prepare yourself, and get in the groove and LISTEN!

14.	Fuel your common hobby. It could be as simple as a soap you both watch together or a passion you both share.

15.	Understand the LD will take its toll on you two, be willing to provide support for each other when the other is in the zone. Encouraging words will suffice.

16.	Enjoy the 'me-time' the long distance affords you. No need feeling guilty about your hanging out with other friends. Don't waste too much energy dwelling on the fact that you aren't together (we already established it's temporary), use the time to build yourself up and develop personal interests.

17.	Shower each other with compliments as often as possible. What's taken for granted will eventually be taken away. Ogle your own.

18.	Finally, decide when this 'separation' will end. Because it must have an expiry date.

LDR may be tough but love sure does conquer all. The thought of you being together again is always something to look forward to. And as long as you both make the effort to make it work, one day you would look back and relish the beauty and the memories the distance gave you.

18

SETTING RIGHT BOUNDARIES

God told Adam, 'You may eat all the fruit except...' Boundaries.

He told Moses 'Six days you shall do all your work, but the 7th day is Sabbath to the Lord, you shall do no work...' Boundaries

He told Satan, "All that he has is in your power; only do not lay a hand on his person." Boundaries.

God has always been big on boundaries.

Abraham was old so he made his servant swear by the God of heaven that he will not take a wife for his son from the daughters of the Canaanites but shall go to his country and to his family and take a wife for his son Isaac. Boundaries

Joseph said 'My master has withheld nothing from me except you. Why? Because you are his wife! Duh! Boundaries

Those who grow and fulfill purpose are those who have identified boundaries in their lives and have been consistent enough to keep them.

Boundaries keep you in check and help you stay on the straight and narrow. For all things are lawful but not all things are expedient. That something does not look sinful does not mean it's helpful.

HOW TO SET BOUNDARIES

1.   *Be self-aware of your goals/dreams/purpose*

If you don't know and acknowledge them, how will you be able to make another respect you?

Where do you stand on certain issues? What is your opinion on topical issues?

Check with yourself, what are your own limits? What are you comfortable or uncomfortable with?

2.   *Communicate your thoughts.*

Once you are certain of what you can take and not take, then share them. Don't assume they know. It might be as simple as, 'I don't like people shouting at me.' or the fact that our friends A and B are in a relationship, and they kiss each other does not mean I am going to do same. Discuss issues, don't assume they know.

3.   *Follow through on what you say.*

Practice what you preach. If you say you don't like it when they use your things without permission, then don't spend the money they keep with you with the excuse that you were planning to return it. That's you making it easy for them to disregard your boundary.

4.   *Take responsibility for your actions or needs.*

It's not because they came late that made you miss the program. It's simply because you didn't plan your time well. Take responsibility. Be responsible for your choices and be willing to take care of your problems. Just be a responsible person. Also borrowing money or other material things often creates a dent on your personality. Live within your means and take responsibility for the things you need. Any little problem, you're already running to them for help. Did they commit a crime by deciding to be your boy/girlfriend?

5. Be responsible.

Expect that there will be a few infractions because we are not all perfect. But never stop reminding them of your preferences. If they err once it's a mistake but if it's becoming a pattern, then something is fundamentally wrong. It's time to have a conversation and review the relationship.

I found some cool boundaries:

- *I like it when you visit. But don't visit after 7pm.*

- *Yes, we can always hug but please don't touch me inappropriately.*

- *Surprises can be quite romantic. But, why is yours mostly unannounced 'stopping by'?*

It's good we are getting freer with each other now. However, kindly inform me first before you take my stuff.

'No' is a complete sentence. You don't have to put a comma and explain. 'No' isn't just a complete sentence, it is a whole paragraph. No means No. It means don't do it, don't come close, don't take it, I refuse to be convinced, I refuse to shift ground. That's a whole paragraph.

Have regard for their boundaries. Respect their safe place. If they say they are uncomfortable about something the very first time, don't smart talk them into reviewing their position. Many times, their first reaction to things are their truest reactions. It's worrisome that the only area you prove your kind of cleverness and brilliance is in prevailing on them to do things they already acknowledged they are uncomfortable with. The only period you show you are 'intelligent and smart' is when it comes to disregarding their set boundaries. That's worrisome.

19

ABUSE IS CANCEROUS

You were never like this!

No! You were never like this!

You had color; you had presence.

Many of us flocked around you because you always had positive vibes.

You had that pull that made people want to know you.

Your laughter was so infectious, you had so bright a light it was blinding.

You were always encouraging, always engaging, always confident, always helpful. You added value. Come on, you were never like this!

You used to be confident. You used to be happy.

You mean they came, and your light suddenly goes dim? That can't be right!

Love was never meant to be a burden.

Love was not meant to do you in.

Love should bring out the best in you.

You mean, this is your best?

A relationship that takes away your sense of dignity and makes you feel less than you are, is not ideal and is definitely not God's plan for you. I don't care how much they profess they love you; I don't care how much material gifts they shower on you, the question remains, is this making you better or is this choking or taking away your essence and purpose?

Abuse creeps in on you slowly you would hardly notice. It's packaged so neatly you could mistake it as affection. It's cancerous. It is invasive. Once it starts, it never stops. Once condoned, it only grows. It could be wrapped in diverse coats of friendliness with a semblance of care that you cannot figure. It makes you become a game for another's controlling habits.

But love is never confusing, love is never uncertain.

Abuse can get you to a place where you begin to justify the abuser's actions by making excuses for them.

It gets you to a point where you conclude you are the problem in the relationship. You believe you are the reason they shout at you. You believe you are the reason they snap at you. You believe you are the reason they misbehave. You conclude you are the problem in the relationship. Your self-esteem drops to an all-time low and you become a shadow of yourself.

How did you get here?

Here is what they do:

They starve you of attention, but they dish it out in generous measures to others.

They belittle your successes but are quick to spot your failings.

They ignore your needs and draw attention to your weaknesses.

They intentionally do things they know so well know you don't like and push your past in your face when you complain.

They disregard your opinions; they ridicule your ideas.

You are constantly frightened when they are around you.

You are forever under a siege to satisfy their inordinate requests.

You are stripped of friends and friendships that are dear to you.

You are threatened when you complain, you are shushed if you dare disapprove.

How did you get here? Just how did you become like this?

You have become a sharp contrast to what you used to be.

You were never like this.

You need to Stop this. You need to Stop now!

You need to Stop this before it completely stops you.

STOP. SEEK HELP.

HELP IS AVAILABLE.

20

ARE THERE PEOPLE ON YOUR LANE?

The red light read 35 seconds as I closed on the Honda CRV in front of me. I put the gear in Park and drank some water. I freed my legs for a little rest, I had 35 seconds, I told myself. I noticed two men a few meters away, all suited up with their laptop bags in hand, chatting passionately. They must be discussing politics looking at how forceful they both fought to make the other listen. My roving eyes left them and perched on the guy inside the car beside me as he munched his burger without any idea he was making me salivate. I stared longingly at him. He took the second bite and my stomach rumbled. I suddenly was hungry. As soon as I noticed he was going to look my way I turned my face, 'No, he didn't see me! Gosh, I pray, he didn't!' The blaring horn behind me brought me back to the peace inside my car. 35 seconds wasn't so long after all. The light had changed to green while I was drooling on another's burger. I quickly changed the gear back to Drive and pressed the horn to wake up the CRV in front of me.

The car didn't move. *It's a lie!*

What?! I pressed the horn harder. At this point all the cars behind me were already blazing their horns. The cab drivers were cursing. *'Abi Olori****** ni man yi ni?!'* *'Carry your jalopy comot for road jor!'* We honked the more.

More abuse flooded in. Naija drivers on Naija roads! Nothing could be more dramatic.

I pressed my horn harder. Then I noticed his indicator beeping left. And we were supposed to be going right as the traffic light indicated. He was not supposed to be on our lane! My annoyance was not printable.

So, I was stuck, we were all stuck behind him. And he couldn't move because there were cars hedging him in. He was going left but stayed on the lane of those turning right. It seemed the realization also dawned on those behind me because though the horns kept blazing, the curses stopped. They knew we were stuck.

I checked the time left for his lane, forty seconds! Forty mighty long seconds!

Anger, frustration, disgust, all manner of negative emotions. And I knew by the time his lane turned green, ours would have changed back to red! I shook my head in utter disappointment.

One of the cab drivers couldn't stomach it. He came out of his car, cursing and fuming, 'Who be this mad man?!' walked past my car and got to the driver side of the CRV.

Yes, his window was wound up. If he heard the man, it was faintly. And he looked away to show him he couldn't be bothered. When he got tired, he left and sorrowfully went back to his car.

"Why are people like this?!"

Those 40 seconds seemed the longest ever – add thirty-eight seconds to it -that was how long my lane had to wait after the CRV had left.

Are there people in your lane?

There are people who just don't know how to stay in their lanes. They are not going in your direction but they cross boundaries and appear in your lane. They are so self-centered, so rude, they wouldn't be bothered they are standing right in front of you, in your lane, blocking your movement and hindering your progress. All they think about is themselves. All they know is their personal interest. Honk hard they won't move. Scream loud they won't bulge. They are so set in their ways, nothing you do will change them.

Are there people in your lane?

They may be cloaked as friends, colleagues, siblings, church members but they are rude and inconsiderate. They subtly sneak in when you are not observing and comfortably position themselves in your front. Or they bully their way in, slow you down, waste your time and make you lose momentum. They know you're frustrated; they see you are irritated, but it only energizes them.

Are there people in your lane?

They come with their unsolicited advice and their I-know-it-all baggage. They cloud your reasoning and make you question your resolve. They assume a role you have not granted them and believe they have the right to speak into your life. They come at you head-long speaking so much you begin to wonder when it was you gave them access. Are there people in your lane?

You may find them anywhere – your family, your office, your neighborhood, your community, your church, your society, name it. They just have a knack of being in your lane. And when they are, it could be difficult to move them.

So, what do you do?

Follow the 3-second rule. The rule simply means you maintain a safe following distance with the car in front of you. That you don't drive too closely, you don't go bumper to bumper, that you allow enough space to create a safety zone in the event of an emergency stop. The rule advises you ensure you can see the bottom of the other driver's wheels, safe enough.

Give yourself room to move around. You must be able to take a rapid, instant move when the need arises.

Maintain a safe following distance, a safety zone, in the event of a recalcitrant selfish driver. You don't want to be stuck, unable to move, by another not going your way.

Don't stay too close. Don't follow too closely. As soon as you notice they have stopped to stop you, use your space, flip on your blinker, and immediately make a right turn. And continue your journey. Their opinion does not matter. Their advice isn't needed. Maneuver and move on.

In the same way, as it applies in driving, it does in relationships. Give everyone space. It's not everyone you do bumper to bumper with. Your journey isn't same. Your destination isn't identical. Sometimes, if not all the time, you need to maintain a safe following distance with people around you. You make a huge mistake when you think you are all on the same assignment. You are not! You are wrong if you think they have all the answers. They don't!

So, give some space and ask, not plead, that it be respected.

You know why?

Because the light won't always be on Red! You won't always be stagnant! You won't always remain in the same spot. You will not be broke forever. You will not be single forever.

Your light will soon turn Green.

And when it does (not, if it does) you sure want to be ready to move without anyone stopping you.

When your light turns Green, you know it is time to move. When it turns Green, you know the wait is over. So, give them space. Don't follow too closely. Don't lean in too heavily. You are about to move!

I am so confident that your light will soon turn green.

You will soon get the job.

You will soon be called upon.

The baby will come.

Your promotion will come.

He will put a ring on it.

You will find love again. Y

our admission is close.

Your victory song is near.

Get ready!

Abuse is cancerous.

It's invasive.

Once it starts, it never stops.

Once condoned, it only grows.

21

LEAVE IT ON REPEAT

I teach my kids new songs in 2 ways:

Directly Intentional (INDI)- I sit in their middle, open the lyrics of the song on YouTube and play it. We play it over and over till they get it.

When I drive them to school or church, or find a free time, I Bluetooth the song and hand my phone over to them to listen some more. They can tell I am pretty much shoving the song down their throat; I want them to learn the song already like yesterday.

Indirectly Intentional (DI)- At home, I put it on Repeat, increase the volume and simply blast it all over the house. I mute the TV, the only sound they hear is the song while they go about their play. They are watching the TV but they are singing 'It's a new level..' They are playing Scrabbles, but they are muttering, *'Awa gbe O ga.'* They are in the kitchen, but they are singing Mavericks' Promises. They can't particularly say I am teaching them a new song; they also can't deny they are learning a new tune.

For *InDI,* they always start out uninterested, unimpressed, and unbothered. But AS TIME GOES ON, with the song on Repeat and them within hearing distance, 3 stages occur.

THE ANNOYANCE STAGE - They're irked with daddy's disturbance; they are pissed with all the noise stopping them from enjoying TV sound. They would like some peace and quiet. And Daddy is being impossible and very annoying.

THE AWARENESS STAGE - My tenacity disarms them. They become aware. Unconsciously, they pick up some lines in the chorus and sing along in mockery. They feel they are ridiculing the song, but they are so nescient of the plot.

THE ACCEPTANCE STAGE - the process fully kicks in; they accept the new situation. They know the lyrics; they own the song. They are hyperaware, hyperconscious, and hyper-assenting. It's engraved in their cerebrum and heedlessly they belt it out without prompting and with careless abandon.

I know they hit the 3rd stage when five hours after I've turned off the music they are still screaming, *'I put my faith in Jesus, my anchor to the ground...'* or 2 days after they are requesting, I play the song again, or a week after they are dissing their mum for getting the lyrics wrong. Time and more time of play, without my direct involvement, and BOOM! It's locked in.

I realized, with the kids, that *DI* sometimes works but *InDI* is more effective. For, many times, it's the indirect exposures that leave a lasting impact. Leave the song to play, and as long as you they are within hearing distance and seeing distance, as long as it's in their vicinity and right there in their neighborhood, the eye-gate and the ear-gate picks it, then the mind-gate locks it in. TIME is the required ingredient.

Shoving it down their throat sometimes stops them and stops you from doing other things. It sometimes comes across like they are being forced to learn it asap and are doing you a favor by learning it. With *InDI*, you press Play, up the volume a bit, wear your Unbothered t-shirt and carry on like nothing is happening. But you're infiltrating the environment with the melody, you are locking all other sounds out and installing a new one, give it time, it will grow on them.

If you don't turn off the music when they consider it a nuisance at first, if you don't allow their disapproval or use of military force to stop or discourage you, if you can bear the wait-time for it to fully mature by leaving it on Repeat, the neurons will transmit the information and the hippocampus part of the brain will do its work. TIME will adroitly seal the deal because Time is the game changer.

Leave it on REPEAT.

22

'BE A LITTLE NICE , DAD'

My daughter got this Connect4 game as gift during the holidays. And immediately, she needed a partner to play it with. She found me and we set about it.

After I won the first game, I took the time and showed her what she was doing wrong that made me win. I explained how she needed to keep one eye on me as I schemed to connect 4 and the other eye on her own strategy to connect her 4. I won the 2nd game. Again, I told her how she missed my plot. And I warned her I wasn't going to play easy just so she could win. I won the 3rd and 4th game. It was 4 -Nil.

My wife got upset. 'What kind of a father are you? Be a little nice and allow the little girl win some.' Her disapproval fell on deaf ears. I won the 5th and 6th game. It was 6-Nil. At that point I felt really bad, like an Agbaya. The sad look on her face made the guilt more excruciating. I wanted us to stop playing but she wanted to still play in the hope that she might just get one win in. So, we played again. I won the 7th and 8th.

I just didn't know how to play her easy and make her win on a platter, I felt it would be cheating and deceptive. She gave up and wouldn't play with me for a while.

Two weeks later we travelled home for the Christmas holidays, and she took the game along. I was in the room when she ran in and jumped on me in excitement announcing how she was winning all her cousins, the 6 of them!

You needed to see the look on her face. The taste of victory had never looked sweeter. I was elated.

What if I had played easy? What if I had allowed her to win me on a platter? This moment was what I would be missing. And the losses she got from two of them, she handled like a champ and played them again till she led the scores. For days my daughter was walking on sunshine.

What you have handed to you on a platter, you don't get the opportunity to master. Whatever comes easy hardly lasts long. Certain losses only prepare you for a bigger win. Don't wish your journey was easier, pray for strength to overcome a difficult one. For stamina, strength and skills are first cousins with hard work, heartbreaks, and disappointments. Victory is sweeter and more fulfilling when you look back at the many losses you had before arriving here.

My daughter and I played again after the holidays. It ended 7-1. You see that one win she got; I cherish it more than the many times I won. And if you ask her, she would only tell you she won Daddy once without telling you the scores.

23

THE EXCITEMENT OF A VIRGIN MIND

Our drive to the airport was fun. We sang. We laughed. And my daughter poked fun at me as I told her the story of how I met her mother. We had just walked into the airport when my daughter beamed with joy knowing fully well, we would be flying DA back to Abuja. She couldn't contain her pleasure. When we came into Lagos with AP, she had complained bitterly she never wanted to fly AP again. What was the problem? 'They are not nice like DA. DA gives us popcorn and treats us well. They are the best.' The endorsement of a 7-year-old.

So, when we told her we booked DA back to Abuja, she hugged us tight, thanked us and announced we were the best parents in the world. She was really looking forward to the flight. She hopped down to her seat in the aircraft, hugged all members of the cabin crew and smiled at some passengers and didn't care if they smiled back or not. My daughter was just ecstatic. Of course she wanted the window seat and that was what she got. She wanted her brother to sit beside her and that we obliged. She buckled her belt and waited to hear the captain's address. I sat behind her and marveled at how she was simply overjoyed with the thought of flying DA.

I don't like flying DA, that's beside the fact that flying doesn't excite me in this country. If I must list 10 airlines of choice, DA won't feature. I think their aircrafts are old and their pilots aren't smooth. And since the crash in 2012 that claimed over a hundred and fifty lives, DA seized to be my airline of choice. They delay flights and even cancel sometimes. I pray more than usual whenever we must fly them. Take off is rough, landing is rougher. No, I am not a fan of DA. But my daughter is.

My daughter didn't know any of my reservations about the airline. She didn't know about the 150+ people that lost their lives years back. She pretty much couldn't tell the difference between good landing and bad landing. Every aircraft was the same to her, they were all big and massive. She hadn't been disappointed by DA. And times when DA delayed her, she took the waiting time as just some extra lunch and hangout time. And because of all these that she was unaware of and disappointments she hadn't faced, inconsistencies she was oblivious of, her excitement for DA was unparalleled. She is trusting. She is believing.

That, for me, is the excitement of a virgin mind. Never known disappointment. Never known any failings. Never been heartbroken. Never been distraught. The virgin mind is goofy and hyper. A little popcorn is sufficient to win their heart. Their innocence is genuine. Their joy is pure and real. Their excitement is very contagious and sometimes upsetting.

You've seen it play out in young loves; you've seen it displayed in first loves. You may preach caution all you care and warn about how we all err; it won't faze them. They won't yield. They are like my 7yr old, they know nothing about the 'plane crashes' that raise your doubts, they know nothing about the important meetings 'delays in flight schedules' make you lose. They can't tell if the 'aircraft' has a funny sound or not, and they can't tell the difference between old and new. Their reality is the popcorn, their reality is the warm and beautiful cabin crew ladies. The excitement of a virgin mind.

I wish I could tell them they won't ever be disappointed. I wish I could tell you not to damage their virgin hearts. I wish I could ask them to tread with caution, I wish I could tell you to handle and treat them well. But they are virgins, and you are human. As their experience is real, so is your folly. So, just as I sat behind my daughter and watch the pure radiance of her soul and the inexplicable peace that radiated her being, I must confess I enjoyed it. I envied her. I wished my mind hadn't been soiled by the harsh realities of life. I wished I could delete the 'crashes,' and the inconsistencies. But I couldn't. Again, I dared not share my gory tales and report how DA is unreliable and unfaithful. That would be me trying to make her become like me. That would be me dragging her into the muddy corner of my weather-beaten heart and wanting her to be sorry and distrusting like me.

When you see or witness the excitement of virgin minds, if you can't share in their joy, and be excited with them, just keep quiet. Allow them to experience the euphoria, for however long or short it lasts. Allow them to feel the purity of their virginity. Don't be quick to warn them about the uncertainties of their love interest and how all men/women are fallible. When they get to that bridge, they would cross it. I mean, didn't you cross yours? They would be fine. Let them be. And for all you know, their story may not always end like yours. You never know, there may be no 'crashes' in their future, and there may be no 'delays in their flights.' Yes, their faith can be that strong. So, stop spreading your sour realities every time you see someone enjoy a new love. Their honeymoon could be for a month, or it could be for two decades or it may even last forever, what is that to you? Let them be! Let them feel. They deserve that experience.

The issue is many of us are so broken, we get mad at others for being whole. We are so damaged; we get irritated when we see pristine. Shouldn't they be allowed their moment? Why steal from them? That's unfair and selfish.

Next time your friend share about their newfound love, be genuinely happy for them, don't sneer.

Next time your friend shares fun stories of their two-month-old baby, we know you've raised 5 kids and you know the phases of child development, keep it quiet and allow them enjoy their moment.

Next time, a new employee is ecstatic about the largesse of the boss, don't be quick to announce how you've been in the company for 5 years and how the boss is not that nice.

Let people enjoy their moments. And for all you care, their moments could actually last forever! I mean, you are not God to decide contrary.

24

REGARDLESS

When my wife and I were courting, I wanted so much to show her how much I loved and valued her. I also wanted everyone to know heaven had smiled on me; the wait was over, and I had found the one. So, I would post her picture on Facebook and would give it a romantic caption. Other times I would simply wax poetic about my love for her. My smile was bigger, my gait was swifter, and my focus became sharper.

If I was in a conversation with you long enough, her name would pop up effortlessly. A day wouldn't go by without me eulogizing her. I was in love, and you bet, I was not shy about it. All my writing and poetry skills artlessly found a medium of expression. It was as if they were hibernating and then Toluwalogo showed up and BOOM! They got freedom to roam.

We got married and the tempo was heightened. Like every other day, I found some romantic thought, some love line to put on my status along with her picture. It was bliss. It was sweet cruise.

After a while, I began to feel that I was the only one this love was 'shacking.' I felt I was the only one, this love was 'doing.' Because she was not expressive and spotlighting as I was, I concluded it was not 'doing' my wife the way it was 'doing' me. And that made me a bit sad and disappointed. And to make matters worse, I would put her picture up with a romantic line and she would not acknowledge it! What?! Four or five days after it had been up, her friends would be the one teasing her about my status, then she would check and see my BBM status. It was then she would come back and say, Thank you. It was very annoying. I felt I was wasting all my love, devotion, and adoration. And I felt what was the point of continuing when the object of my love did not even care about my effort and the work I was putting in.

I told myself, "No more!" And I stopped. I stopped the FB posts. I stopped the BBM status thingy. I stopped writing. I just didn't want to do them anymore. I mean, what was the point? She wasn't even noticing.

Guess what? I stopped and she didn't notice I stopped!! She didn't! You know how you stop doing something just to get someone's attention and probably make them to act better. I tried it. It didn't work. My wife didn't feel or notice anything. Her life continued. Nothing changed. Nothing felt different. More frustrating was the fact that by stopping, I felt like fish out of water. I wasn't myself. I was (am) naturally expressive and not being able to express myself felt like being imprisoned. I felt like a nursing mother whose breast was full of milk but had no child to breastfeed.

It was while I was in that state that I asked myself several pertinent questions. "Were you doing all you did just for praise and appreciation? Was it all for attention or accolades? What was your motivation really? Why do you do what you do?" My answers changed my perspective and attitude forever.

Have you seen a nursing mother with full breastmilk and her baby not feeding as much as they need to? She is uncomfortable. She is restless. The breast aches. It could lead to mastitis or abscess. She would search the house for bottles to express the milk into. She finds a release, regardless of the baby's need for milk. Why? Because when you are full, you let out and release, regardless.

I imagine a Christian is like a nursing mother full of breastmilk; full of love to give, as bestowed upon us by God. Full of kindness, full of faith, full of joy, full of compassion, full of godly character. Such are the things we are full of. By default, those are the virtues we release. At conversion, we received a new setting. We were translated from darkness to light. So, all that Light is about is programmed into us.

So we are wired to give, regardless.

It's okay for your goodness to be acknowledged, but Regardless, we remain good.

It's not bad to want your kindness reciprocated, but Regardless, we stay kind.

It's nice to know your commendation was noticed but Regardless, we continue to give.

Whether I get their reaction or not, whether they notice it or not. Whether they requite it or not, whether they even the score or not. In any case, in any way, we do it Regardless.

There are character traits God has worked in you over the years. There are trainings He has given you through the ages that have turned you into the person that you are today. Your personality is not by happenstance, it's a testament of your walk and relationship with God. When you take your personae into a relationship, it's abnormal to make the other a remote control that determines when you are to be kind or not. Your partner is not some device or mechanism that turns you from sweet to sour. If that happens, maybe you really were not a sweet person in the first place.

It took me two years after marriage to accept that my wife was/is not the PDA type or a social media person. I had thought every woman was. So, I was expecting from her what she was not wired to give, and I was trying to force my love expressions on her. It didn't work.

I wish I could tell you that ten years after, she is now acknowledging my PDA gestures and reciprocating in SAME measure as regards my style of expressing love. I wish. Of course, there has been tremendous conscious effort and progress from her, however, she is not me; our personalities are different. Her personality and essence remain true. Her style is different and that I have grown to embrace. She is private, a behind-the-scenes kind of person. Very furtive and off screen. She is effusive in her love, but she is also esoteric with it. It dawned on me it really doesn't have to be as I show it. She really doesn't have to be like me to love me. And I really don't have to look out for her response to love her like I should. We love, regardless.

Marriage is not 50-50. It's not, when she uses my picture as DP, then I will use hers as DP. It's not, when she buys me a shirt, then I will buy her a skirt. It's not, she didn't give me a gift on my birthday, she shouldn't expect anything on hers. Grow up! Marriage isn't that!

Marriage is John 13:34 "As I have loved you, so you must love one another." How has Christ loved you?

While you were dead in sin, He died for you. That's how. While you were undeserving, He shed His blood. That's how. And even now that He has saved you, you still continue to mess up, but His love remains Constant. That's how. He didn't wait for you to straighten up before He chose you, He's not waiting for you to have it all together before He helps you. He loves you REGARDLESS.

Christ is your measuring standard for doing anything to and for your spouse.

So, when you wax romantic, do it Regardless.

When you give, do it Regardless.

When you care, do it Regardless.

When you love, do it Regardless.

Do it because the Father has lots and lots of deposit in you and your default setting is to release out of the abundance you have received. Love, regardless.

A little brown cork fell in the path of a whale who lashed it down with its angry tail. But, despite the blows, it quickly arose and floated serenely before his nose. Said the cork to the whale, "You may flap and sputter and frown, but you never can keep me down. For I'm made of stuff that is buoyant enough to float instead of to drown."

As a Christian, you are made of stuff that is powerful and transformative enough to love than to hate or be spiteful. Your genetic code carries Christ and that is what predetermines your actions and reactions. When a man and a woman have this understanding and mindset and come together in a marital relationship, the resultant marriage is a beauty to behold. When husband is resolved to do 100% and wife is also on that resolve, what they have is a healthy competition to outdo each other in love.

A story is told of a weary traveler who was passing along a lonely roadway and noticed in his path a dry, shriveled leaf. Picking it up, he was amazed at the lovely perfume it exuded.

"Oh, you poor withered leaf," he exclaimed, "whence comes this exquisite perfume?"

The leaf replied, "I have lain for a long time in the company of a rose."

Be a rose. Love, regardless.

25

BUT IT'S NOT RED

From the time I was knee-high as a grasshopper we had always used Close Up Red as toothpaste. That was what my siblings and I grew up with. My mum never tried another. Our tongue never tasted other. Red was it.

University days after, NYSC days after, marriage after, children after, decades after, Red has been it. I think it's only my brother that made a switch to Colgate. Just thinking about it now, I should ask him why he changed and at what point he changed. But I could easily make a guess why.

Anyway, I was in the supermarket one fateful day to pick a few things for the house and toothpaste was one of the items needed. I didn't find Red. Very unusual. I searched and didn't find. I went to the salesperson and asked and she said they ran out of stock. I had picked all other things I needed save toothpaste. I turned my head sideways for some seconds, I checked other variations they had, I picked them up and turned them over one after the other. I thought. I reconsidered. I contemplated. Then I decided. I picked the next variation of it, I picked Herbal. Come on, it's the same product, isn't it?

How many times do we do that with different things in our lives? I'm getting ahead of myself.

The following morning, my wife jolted me from the bathroom, "Olami! What is this?"

I lifted my head to see her poke hers out from the bathroom. "What?"

"What kind of toothpaste is this?" She asked with foam in her mouth. "Close Up."

"It's not Red!" She spat it out. "Apparently."

"Why didn't you buy Red?"

"Because they didn't have. It's out of stock."

"Who didn't have? Out of stock in all shops or in shop A."

"Shop A didn't have." I continued what I was doing. Of course, I had no proof other shops didn't have.

"Did you check other shops? Like shops B, C, D, E, F, G, H I J K L M N O..." She wouldn't let up.

"Baby!"

"Come and use it before you Babied me!" "But it's still Close Up now!"

"But it's not Red!"

She mumbled other things I didn't hear and didn't bother to hear.

I didn't find Red in the place I thought and expected to find it, that's why I chose Herbal. I was lazy to make some five minutes' drive to check shops B or C or D for Red. I didn't, so I chose Herbal. The problem isn't that the manufacturer failed to supply Red into the market. I was the one who didn't make effort to check other places. It wasn't that the salesperson said other shops didn't have Red, I was the one who chose Herbal.

What's your Red that you have compromised for Herbal? What are you not making effort to get that you are settling for less? Of course, there are those who like

Herbal, those who use Herbal, those who would pick Herbal any day over Red. I mean, that's why it's in the market, it has its customers. But that's not you, and you know. Are you settling just because of 'a five minutes' drive' to get your Red? Are you reviewing, reconsidering, deliberating, ruminating, turning other variations over and over, justifying, just because you wouldn't try some other place?

Herbal may be available; it doesn't mean Red isn't obtainable.

And if you bring Herbal home, my wife has this to say, "But it's not Red!"

I was in the bathroom the next day. I was about picking my toothbrush and then I saw Red. I don't know what my wife did with my Herbal but it was no longer there. I saw Red. And I used Red.

26

JUST SPEAK!

As you both set out in the morning.

Ready to pour yourself into your work.

Wait a minute, slow down a second.

Don't leave the room just yet.

Hold her hands. Place yours in his.

You may even hug, I mean, you are a couple!

Say a short prayer. Speak a blessing.

Speak into her day. Prophesy into his day.

Don't make it long, keep it short.

In that connection and strong link

Agree together on what the day would be.

Establish for yourselves how you want it.

The lines fall for him in pleasant places

Jehovah shields her continually with favor.

The Hand of God be upon her for good.

The Spirit of excellence rests upon him.

He makes right decisions to-day

Her heart indicts of a good matter all day.

Sovereign God garrisons her heart with peace.

 The Almighty keeps him from all evil.

Say it. Speak it. Declare it.

Do it on Monday.

Make it happen on Tuesday.

Show up on Wednesday.

Report on Thursday.

Thank God it's Friday.

Saturday's got nothing on you.

It's a new page on Sunday.

It's not in the length of the prayer, it's in the consistency.

It's not in the loudness of the petition, it's in the commitment to it.

It's less than 60 seconds but it's more potent than 60 'prayer prophets'

Its effect is long-lasting. The rewards are unquantifiable.

So, before you set out tomorrow morning

Before you rush out to work before sunrise

Hold her hands. Join your hands with him

And speak. Just speak. Just say it as you want it.

Before you get out of that door

Decide what happens behind the door.

You don't have to feel like it. Just speak.

You don't have to be in the mood. Just speak.

Let your feelings catch up with your speakings

Let your mood line up with your declarations.

Do it till you feel it.

Say it till you believe it

Just speak!

Stand in the middle of that room and let your mouth

dance

Let it dance to the rhythm of your desired future

Let it sing the song of your expectations.

Open your mouth and speak!

And week in week out, you are sowing seeds

Week in week out you are making deposits.

The results may not be readily evident

The rewards may not be immediate

But like seeds, they are taking roots deep inside.

And the shoots will come out in a matter of time

First the blade, then the ear, then the full grain

It will be visible. It will be evident.

First visible signs,

sickness leaves you abode, hospital runs seize.

Peace unimaginable envelopes your home.

Progress unprecedented saturate your lives

Your love grows.

Your bond thickens.

Your tie becomes stronger.

Your communication gets better.

Your intimacy peaks to new levels.

Before you get out of that door tomorrow morning Decide
what happens outside the door!

It's not in the loudness of the petition, it's in the commitment to it.

It's less than 60 seconds but it's more potent than 60 'prayer prophets'

Its effect is long-lasting. The rewards are unquantifiable. Before you get out of that door tomorrow morning Decide what happens outside the door!

Final Note

Your downtime today

are the very materials needed for your next song

Trust the process.

The 'hell' you're going through now

are the stuff breakthroughs are made of.

Trust the process.

Be aware of the flow.

Pay attention to details.

Document the various phases.

Take note of the characters involved.

Capture the scenes, archive all the episodes.

Because, very soon, the whole script will make sense And then we will ask you to tell us how you got here.

It will all add up in the end. The spotlight will soon be on you.

Trust the process.It's not in the length of the prayer, it's in the consistency.

ABOUT THE AUTHOR

Juwon Odutayo, certified Family Therapist, teacher, trainer, is the husband of Toluwalogo and the father of Ayanfe and Afooreofe.

@juwonodutayo
odutayojuwon@gmail.com
www.juwonodutayo.com

RANDOM REFLECTIONS